FANTASY FOOTBALL

by Michael Decker

The **Greater** World of **Sports**

SportsZone

An Imprint of Abdo Publishing | abdobooks.com

abdobooks.com

Published by Abdo Publishing, a division of ABDO, PO Box 398166, Minneapolis, Minnesota 55439. Copyright © 2020 by Abdo Consulting Group, Inc. International copyrights reserved in all countries. No part of this book may be reproduced in any form without written permission from the publisher. SportsZone™ is a trademark and logo of Abdo Publishing.

Printed in the United States of America, North Mankato, Minnesota
102019
012020

Cover Photos: iStockphoto, football, notepad
Interior Photos: Randy Shropshire/Getty Images Entertainment/Getty Images, 5, 6; John Sleezer/Kansas City Star/Tribune News Service/Getty Images, 9; iStockphoto, 11, 18, 24 (football); Anda Chu/Contra Costa Times/Bay Area News Group/Tribune News Service/Getty Images, 12; Shutterstock Images, 14; Tim Bedison/Fort Worth Star-Telegram/MCT/Tribune News Service/Getty Images, 17; Bruce Kluckhohn/AP Images, 21; WENN Rights Ltd/Alamy, 22; Red Line Editorial, 24–25 (charts); Bruce Kluckhohn/AP/Rex Features, 27; Mark Von Holden/Sirius XM Radio/Getty Images Entertainment/Getty Images, 28

Editor: Melissa York
Series Designer: Melissa Martin

Library of Congress Control Number: 2019942080

Publisher's Cataloging—in—Publication Data

Names: Decker, Michael, author
Title: Fantasy Football / by Michael Decker
Description: Minneapolis, Minnesota : Abdo Publishing, 2020 | Series: The greater world of sports | Includes online resources and index
Identifiers: ISBN 9781532190391 (lib. bdg.) | ISBN 9781532176241 (ebook)
Subjects: LCSH: Fantasy football (Game)--Juvenile literature. | Fantasy sports--Juvenile literature. | Owner simulations (Fantasy sports)--Juvenile literature. | Football fans--Juvenile literature. | American football--Juvenile literature. | Sports--Juvenile literature.
Classification: DDC 796.332640--dc23

TABLE OF CONTENTS

Chapter 1

TIME TO
DRAFT

A group of 12 team owners gathers around the table. Computers, papers, and pens cover the flat surface. The owners all take their seats. In just moments, the action will begin.

It's mid-August, and the owners have assembled to hold their annual fantasy football draft. They prepared by tracking how National Football League (NFL) players did the previous season and studying new players who have come into the league. Finally, they are ready to select players for the upcoming season.

Sam has the first pick in the draft. She quickly announces she is taking New York Giants running

Often friends gather at the beginning of the season to draft their fantasy football teams.

back Saquon Barkley. After Sam is done, Zach selects Alvin Kamara, a running back for the New Orleans Saints. Each fantasy football team owner gets to select one NFL player in the first round of the draft.

Some leagues keep track of draft picks on a large poster.

Later in the first round, Michaela gets a chance to select the first player for her team. She yells out "Patrick Mahomes from the Kansas City Chiefs!" Taylor groans. He wanted the Chiefs quarterback, but Michaela was earlier in the draft order. Michaela believes Mahomes will score many points this year, between his rushing and passing yards and touchdowns.

Now Taylor will have to shift his pick to another player. This happens a lot in fantasy football drafts. Owners constantly reorganize the list of players they want to draft, check who is still available, and furiously scribble down new choices.

For the next few hours, the team owners take turns adding more players to their rosters. Early in the draft, quarterbacks, running backs, and wide receivers are the top targets. The elite players in those positions are expected to score a lot of points, so they go quickly in the draft.

By the end, tight ends, kickers, and team defenses start going fast. Owners also choose backups to the players they drafted earlier. Backups are used when a starter is injured or has a week off. After 12 rounds have been completed, the draft ends.

Different Types of Leagues

Many fantasy football leagues require players to draft an entirely new team each year. But that isn't always the case. Some leagues are known as keeper leagues or dynasty leagues. In these types of leagues, owners can keep a certain number of players from the previous year's roster.

Following the draft, the owners await the start of the NFL season. Once the season begins, everyone in the league tries to win as many games as possible and make the playoffs. The goal

A good quarterback can help a fantasy team owner score a lot of points each week.

is the championship trophy and a year's worth of bragging rights.

People have been playing fantasy football since as far back as the 1960s. The sport is a great way for fans to stay involved with the NFL and cheer on players throughout the whole league.

Chapter 2

FANTASY'S HISTORY

The first version of fantasy football was created in the 1960s by Bill Winkenbach, a part owner of the Oakland Raiders. Earlier, he had created a simple version of fantasy golf, in which owners drafted pro players each week and the person with the lowest score won. With two friends, Winkenbach built on that idea to create rules for fantasy football in 1962.

The Oakland owner only allowed people who worked closely with the team or had season tickets to the Raiders to join his league. They called it the Greater Oakland Professional Pigskin Prognosticators League. The league had many

Fantasy football was played entirely on paper at first.

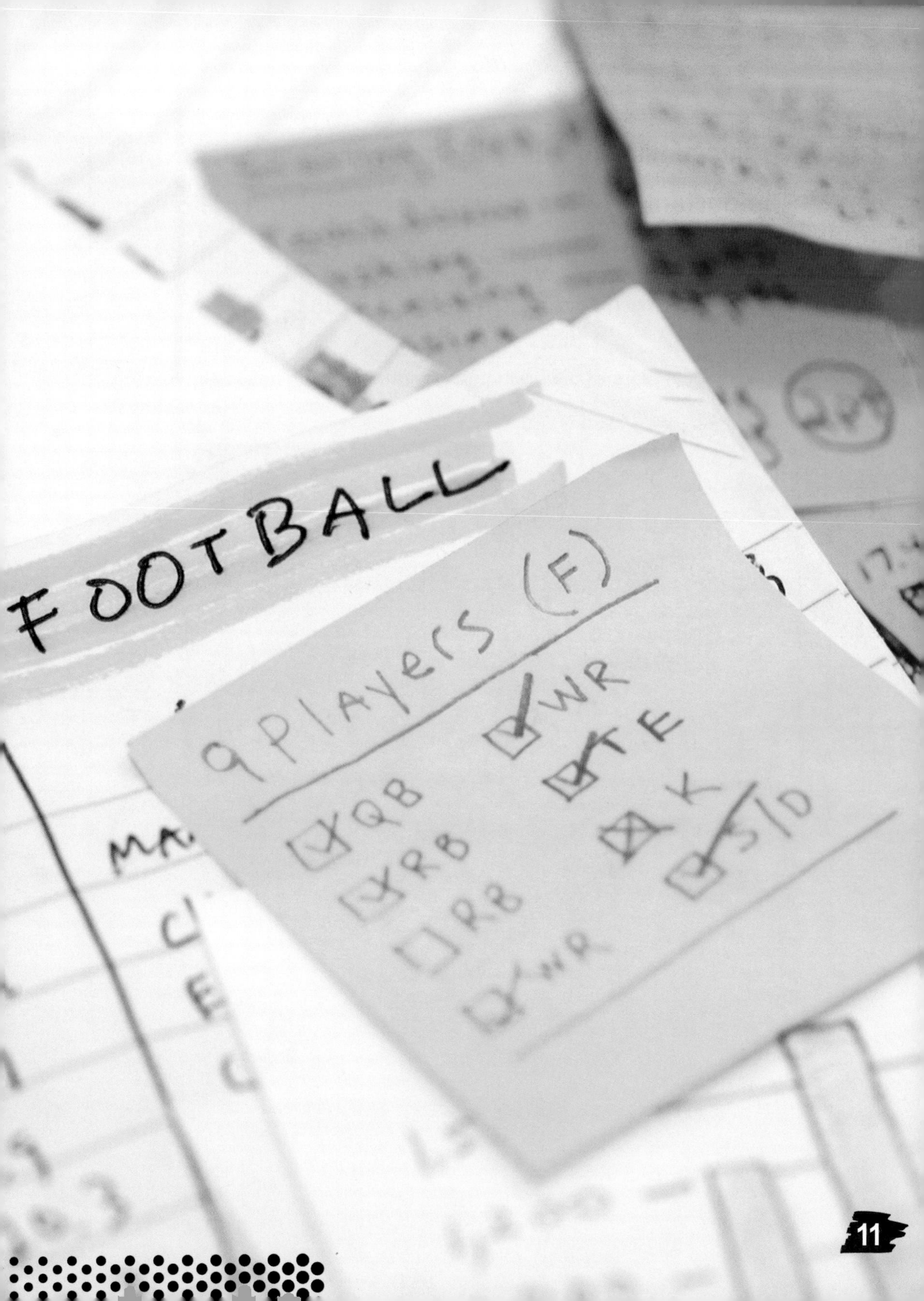
FOOTBALL
9 Players (F)
QB
RB
RB
WR
WR
TE
K
S/D

rules similar to today's fantasy football rules. One important difference was this league only allowed points for touchdowns. Unlike in today's game, yards were not used in scorekeeping.

Some members of the first fantasy football league have been playing for decades.

Unlike today, all of the scoring and other tracking was done by hand. Owners looked up the statistics in the newspapers and did all the math on their own. It took hours to keep up with what was happening in the NFL.

Over the years, other people began to play fantasy football. In 1984, a pair of friends from Minnesota put out a fantasy football manual that made it easier for team owners to track down information about NFL players and their fantasy football stats from previous years.

Daily Fantasy Football

Daily fantasy football has been growing in popularity since its debut in 2007. Like traditional fantasy football, owners select a quarterback, running back, and other position players. Then team owners compete against each other. The owner with the most points that week wins. Owners select a new team each week.

Fantasy Football

NFL Enterprises LLC

3+

26 MB

INSTALL

Contains ads

When the internet became more widely available in the 1990s, fans could pay to participate in fantasy football online. Many websites automatically tracked and added up statistics, making it easier for owners to keep up with the action.

In 1999 Yahoo! became the first major website to offer fans free online fantasy football. These changes helped increase the popularity of fantasy football even more.

Today there are many apps for playing fantasy football online.

Chapter 3

HOW THE GAME WORKS

The most important component of many fantasy football leagues is the commissioner. This person is the head of the league. He or she sets up the draft, establishes the scoring system, and makes sure when owners trade players that the deals are fair for both sides.

Leagues vary in the number of owners that participate. Most leagues have eight to 14 teams. Owners then usually draft 12 to 14 players. While many leagues use similar scoring systems, it's up to each league to set its own rules. Like real football, the goal is to outscore the opponent.

Some people get very involved in their fantasy football teams.

The draft can happen either in person or online. The order of the draft might be determined with a random draw. Other leagues may set the order based on how the teams finished the previous year.

Some people take many notes to prepare for the draft.

Once the order is set, the draft can begin. Many leagues use a snake draft. This means the order flips each round. The team owner with the top pick in round one then has the last pick in round two. The order alternates for the rest of the draft.

Once the draft is over, it's on to the season. Each week teams set their lineups. Owners can only start a certain number of players. Many leagues allow owners to start a quarterback, two running backs, two wide receivers, a tight end, a kicker, and a defense. Some leagues also have a flex position. Owners can start either a running back, wide receiver, or tight end at this spot. Owners can change their lineups each week. Owners often switch their players depending on which NFL teams are competing. They swap out players who are injured, facing a tough defense, or having a bye week.

Owners can also add unsigned players to their teams. This happens during the waiver period, which is the middle of each week while no games are being played. A system determines which owner has the first claim on these free players. In return, the owner must drop a player from his or her roster. Owners can also agree to trade players. In some leagues, other owners can stop a trade if they think it will be unfair.

Some leagues only award points when a player scores a touchdown, a field goal, or an extra point. Those are called scoring-only leagues. In many other leagues, each position also gets points for certain actions. For example, quarterbacks might get a point for every 25 passing yards. Other positions can earn points for yards gained. Defenses can gain points from sacks, interceptions, forced fumbles, recovered fumbles, or how many points they allow.

Owners may need to change their lineups if a star player is injured or not playing.

Near the end of the NFL regular season, the fantasy playoffs begin. These playoffs usually take three weeks of play to finish. The top eight owners' teams in the league often make the playoffs. They face off against each other during the last three weeks. In the end, one team is crowned champion.

Points Per Reception

In some leagues, players earn a certain point total for each catch they make. These leagues are called Points Per Reception (PPR) leagues. In other leagues, players do not earn any additional points for each reception.

Even celebrities such as actor Ashton Kutcher get caught up in fantasy football.

SCORING SYSTEM

This is a basic scoring system that puts an equal emphasis on scoring and yardage, also called a 50/50 system.

Offense
Passing Yards: 1 point per 50 yards
Passing Touchdowns: 4 points
Rushing/Receiving Yards: 1 point per 20 yards
Rushing/Receiving Touchdowns: 6 points

Kickers
Point After Touchdown Kick: 1 point
Field Goal: 3 points

Defense/Special Teams
Safety: 2 points
Fumble Recovery: 1 point
Interception: 1 point
Sack: 1 point
0 Points Allowed: 6 points
1–9 Points Allowed: 4 points
10–19 Points Allowed: 2 points

Position	Player 1	Statistics (points)	Fantasy Points	Player 2	Statistics (points)	Fantasy Points
QB	Mahomes KC	256 pass yds (5) 21 rush yds (1) 4 pass TDs (16)	22	Brees NO	439 pass yds (8) 3 pass TDs (12)	20
RB	Barkley NYG	106 rush yds (5) 22 rec yds (1) 1 rush TD (6)	12	Elliott DAL	69 rush yds (3) 17 rec yds (0) 1 rush TD (6)	9
RB	Gordon LAC	64 rush yds (3) 102 rec yds (5)	8	Gurley LAR	108 rush yds (5) 39 rec yds (1) 1 rec TD (6)	12
WR	Jones ATL	169 rec yds (8) 11 rush yds (0)	8	Green CIN	92 rec yds (4) 1 rec TD (6)	10
WR	Evans TB	147 rec yds (7) 1 rec TD (6)	13	Thielen MIN	102 rec yds (5)	5
TE	Gronkowski NE	123 rec yds (6) 1 rec TD (6)	12	Ertz PHI	48 rec yds (2)	2
K	Tucker BAL	5 PATs (5) 2 FGs (6)	11	Vinatieri IND	2 PATs (2) 3 FGs (9)	11
D/ST	Panthers	1 fumble (1) 6 sacks (6) 8 pts allowed (4)	11	Texans	2 fumbles (2) 1 interception (1) 2 sacks (2)	5
Final Score			97			74

Chapter 4

PART OF
THE SPORT

Fans around the world are making fantasy football more and more popular. Fans play with people they know, or they can join a league on the internet and play with other football fans near and far.

Almost all fantasy football leagues today are scored online. Fans can search the internet and finds countless articles that rank the best players at each position and get advice each week on which players to start and which players to leave on the bench.

Fantasy owners have hundreds of resources to choose from to play fantasy football today.

Playing fantasy football can make people bigger fans of professional football.

Many TV and radio shows broadcast news about fantasy football.

Since Yahoo! first offered free fantasy football, many other sites have also created their own versions.

During NFL games, many fans spend a lot of time tracking how their fantasy team is doing. They might watch a game that doesn't feature their home team just so they can see how one of their fantasy players is doing. Fans can use their phones or tablets to track their fantasy team results as the games are happening. They can also adjust their rosters and chat with friends about the games that are going on. Fans who attend NFL games can watch highlights of other games on stadium scoreboards.

Approximately 12.5 million fans played fantasy football in 2017. That number has increased by more than 5 million since 2012. More and more people are joining the world of fantasy football. It's just one more way to get fans interested in the NFL.

Watch and Learn

Today, fantasy football owners can catch up on information about fantasy football at nearly all hours of the day. TV networks such as ESPN have shows that focus specifically on fantasy football. There are also dozens of podcasts in which analysts talk about different players and give advice to owners.

GLOSSARY

analyst

In a broadcast, a person who provides details or explanations specific to the topic.

bye week

A week during the season in which a team doesn't have a game; NFL teams get one bye week each year.

commissioner

The chief executive of a sports league.

draft

A system that allows teams to acquire new players coming into a league.

highlights

An edited collection of video or audio clips that cover the most important or exciting part of a sporting event.

interception

A pass intended for an offensive player that is caught by a defensive player.

league

A group of teams that participate together in a sport.

playoffs

A set of games played after the regular season that decides which team is the champion.

quarterback

The player who directs the offense and throws the ball.

roster

A list of players that make up a team.

sack

A tackle of the quarterback behind the line of scrimmage before he can pass the ball.

statistics

A collection of numbers or data.

MORE INFORMATION

BOOKS

Gray, Aaron Jonathan. *Football Record Breakers*. Minneapolis, MN: Abdo Publishing, 2016.

Martin, Brett S. *STEM in Football*. Minneapolis, MN: Abdo Publishing, 2018.

Wilner, Barry. *Total Football*. Minneapolis, MN: Abdo Publishing, 2017.

ONLINE RESOURCES

To learn more about fantasy football, please visit **abdobooklinks.com** or scan this QR code. These links are routinely monitored and updated to provide the most current information available.

INDEX

ABOUT THE AUTHOR

Michael Decker has spent his career as a children's book author, writing about various topics. He lives in Wyoming.